WORLD IN
FOCUS

FOCUS ON
GERMANY

DAVID FLINT

WORLD ALMANAC® LIBRARY

Please visit our web site at: www.worldalmanaclibrary.com
For a free color catalog describing World Almanac® Library's list of high-quality books
and multimedia programs, call 1-800-848-2928 (USA) or 1-800-387-3178 (Canada).
World Almanac® Library's fax: (414) 332-3567.

Library of Congress Cataloging-in-Publication Data available upon request from publisher.
Fax (414) 336-0157 for the attention of the Publishing Records Department.

ISBN 0-8368-6218-X (lib. bdg.)
ISBN 0-8368-6237-6 (softcover)

This North American edition first published in 2006 by
World Almanac® Library
A Member of the WRC Media Family of Companies
330 West Olive Street, Suite 100
Milwaukee, WI 53212 USA

Commissioning editor: Victoria Brooker
Editor: Patience Coster
Inside design: Chris Halls, www.mindseyedesign.co.uk
Cover design: Hodder Wayland
Series concept and project management by EASI-Educational Resourcing (info@easi-er.co.uk)
Statistical research: Anna Bowden

World Almanac® Library editor: Alan Wachtel
World Almanac® Library cover design: Scott Krall

Population Density Map © 2003 UT-Battelle, LLC. All rights reserved.
Data for population density maps reproduced under licence from UT-Battelle, LLC.
All rights reserved.
Maps and graphs: Martin Darlison, Encompass Graphics

Picture acknowledgements:
The author and publisher would like to thank the following for allowing their pictures to be
reproduced in this publication:
Corbis 8 (Archivo Iconografico, S. A.), 21 (Alex Grimm/Reuters), 22 (Brooks Kraft), 24 (Owen
Franken), 34 (Reuters), 37 (Reuters), 44 (Fabrizio Bensch), 52 (Ken Straiton), 56 (Bossu Regis);
EASI-Images/Edward Parker cover, 4, 5, 6, 9, 10, 11, 12, 13, 14, 15, 16, 17, 18, 19, 20, 23, 25, 26,
27, 28, 29, 30, 31, 32, 33, 35, 36, 38, 39, 40, 41, 42, 43, 45, 46 and title page, 47, 48, 49, 50, 51,
53, 54, 55, 57, 58 and 59.

The directional arrow portrayed on the map on page 7 provides only an approximation of north.
The data used to produce the graphics and data panels in this title were the latest available at the
time of production.

Printed in China

1 2 3 4 5 6 7 8 9 10 09 08 07 06

CONTENTS

1 Germany – An Overview   4

2 History   8

3 Landscape and Climate   14

4 Population and Settlements   18

5 Government and Politics   22

6 Energy and Resources   26

7 Economy and Income   30

8 Global Connections   34

9 Transportation and Communications   38

10 Education and Health   42

11 Culture and Religion   46

12 Leisure and Tourism   50

13 Environment and Conservation   54

14 Future Challenges   58

Time Line   60

Glossary   61

Further Information   62

Index   63

Cover: A busy street in Heidelberg.

Title page: Young people enjoy May Day in Bavaria.

CHAPTER 1

Germany – An Overview

Germany is a large, economically powerful and important country at the heart of Europe. It has close links with its neighbors, and it is a leading member of the European Union (EU). Germany extends about 497 miles (800 kilometers) from the Baltic coast and North Sea in the north to the borders of Austria and Switzerland in the south. It extends about 435 miles (700 km) from the borders of France, Belgium, and the Netherlands in the west to the borders of Poland and the Czech Republic in the east. It covers a total area of 137,846 square miles (357,021 square kilometers), which makes it slightly smaller than the state of Montana.

GERMANY'S DEVELOPMENT AS A NATION

As a result of its history, culture, and politics, Germany has had a greater impact on Europe than any other country on the continent. In the nineteenth century, Germany was unified under Otto von Bismarck, the leader of the state of Prussia. Bismarck waged war against Denmark in 1864 and against Austria in 1866 to create the North German Confederation. In 1871, he added South Germany to this region

▼ The new Olympic stadium in the foreground of this photo of Berlin confirms the continued growth and importance of the capital city of German.

to create what is now known as modern Germany. During the nineteenth century, this area enjoyed great economic success because of its natural resources of coal, iron, and lignite, which were used to develop steel, chemical, and engineering industries.

During the twentieth century, Germany fought and lost two world wars and was divided into two separate countries—East Germany and West Germany—after World War II. In 1990, the two countries were reunited. Today, integration is proceeding rapidly, but there are still major differences between the eastern and western parts of the country. In the eastern region, for example, huge cooperative farms are more common, while in the western region, farms are more often smaller and more traditional.

INDUSTRY AND THE ECONOMY

During the twentieth century, the German economy grew rapidly. This was the result of government directives that managed to harness the country's rich resources. The German economy is now so large and powerful that it is central to the development of Europe as a whole. Germany has brought about some of the most advanced and innovative industrial developments ever. German manufactured goods, such as cars and electronics equipment, are sold all over the

▲ Southern Germany, particularly the state of Bavaria, is dotted with farms and small villages that are separated by areas of dense forest.

world, and Germany is a major world importer of goods such as timber and textiles.

MOUNTAINS, CASTLES, AND CITIES

Germany is famous for its beautiful landscapes, from the mountains of Bavaria in the south to the sand dunes of the Baltic coast in the north. The country has fabulous castles perched on top of steep hillsides above rivers such as the Rhine and the Elbe. There are historic small villages and beautiful stretches of countryside, especially in the Black Forest area in the country's southern region. German cities are vibrant, multicultural, and progressive. They are evolving rapidly, especially in the case of the capital, Berlin, with its numerous new buildings. There are also many great German museums and architectural gems, the result of two thousand years of history.

REMARKABLE GERMANS

Culturally, Germany has produced a wealth of extraordinarily talented people, including the musical composers Johann Sebastian Bach and Ludwig von Beethoven, the writers Johann Wolfgang von Goethe and Fredrich von Schiller, the scientist Albert Einstein, the philosophers Martin Heidegger and Immanuel Kant, and the political writer Karl Marx.

Physical Geography Data

- Land area: 134,835 sq miles/349,223 sq km
- Water area: 3,011 sq miles/7,798 sq km
- Total area: 137,846 sq miles/357,021 sq km
- World rank (by area): 62
- Land boundaries: 2,249 miles/3,620 km
- Border countries: Austria, Belgium, Czech Republic, Denmark, France, Luxembourg, Netherlands, Poland, Switzerland
- Coastline: 1,484 miles/2,388 km
- Highest point: Zugspitze (9,721 ft/2,963 m)
- Lowest point: Neuendorf bei Wilster (-11.6 ft/-3.54 m)

Source: CIA World Factbook

◀ With its narrow streets and baroque churches and buildings, Heidelberg is typical of the older German cities.

DENMARK

Baltic Sea

North Sea

Kiel

SCHLESWIG-
HOLSTEIN

Rostock

Lübeck

Rügen Island

MECKLENBURG-
VORPOMMERN

HAMBURG

Hamburg

POLAND

BREMEN

Bremen

Oldenburg

Elbe

NIEDERSACHSEN

BERLIN ★ BERLIN

Weser

Hannover

Braunschweig

Potsdam

NETHERLANDS

Magdeburg

BRANDENBURG

Münster

Bielefeld

SACHSEN-
ANHALT

NORDRHEIN-WESTFALEN

Hamm

Gelsenkirchen

Dortmund

Göttingen

Elbe

Duisburg

Bochum

Halle

Leipzig

Essen

Ruhr

Krefeld

Wuppertal

Kassel

Dresden

Mönchengladbach

Düsseldorf

GERMANY

SACHSEN

Cologne

Erfurt

Chemnitz

Aachen

Bonn

THURINGEN

HESSEN

ERZGEBIRG

BELGIUM

Rhine

Mosel

CZECH
REPUBLIC

Wiesbaden

**Frankfurt
am Main**

RHEINLAND-
PFALZ

Mainz

Würzburg

LUXEMBOURG

Worms

SAARLAND

Mannheim

Heidelberg

Nuremberg

FRÄNKISCHE ALB

BOHEMIAN FOREST

Saarbrücken

Karlsruhe

BAYERN

Danube

Danube

Stuttgart

Baden Baden

SCHWÄBISCHE ALB

Ulm

Augsburg

FRANCE

Rhine

BLACK FOREST

Freiburg

BADEN-
WURTTEMBERG

Munich

BAVARIA

Lake Constance

BAVARIAN ALPS

Zugspitze
2,963m ▲

SWITZERLAND   LEICHTENSTIEN

AUSTRIA

Legend

★ Capital

● Cities > 1,000,000

● Cities > 500,000

• Other cities

▲ Mountain

N

0 50 100 kilometers

0 50 100 miles

CHAPTER 2

History

The earliest inhabitants of Germany were Celts. In the fourth century B.C., the Celts were gradually displaced by fair-haired Scandinavian tribes from the north and west and Slavic tribes from the east.

THE HOLY ROMAN EMPIRE

In 58 B.C., the Romans occupied the western banks of the Rhine. In A.D. 436, tribes led by Attila the Hun (c.406–453) helped to defeat the Romans. Germany was subsequently divided up and ruled by tribal leaders. In the eighth century, the king of the Franks, Charlemagne (c.742–814), united by force much of what is present-day France and Germany. When Charlemagne died, his empire was broken up. In 962, the eastern part of this old empire became the Holy Roman Empire, which lasted until 1806. The Holy Roman Empire was a loose assembly of states. It gained its name because, from Charlemagne onward, the kings of this territory protected the Christian authority of the pope in Rome.

THE REFORMATION

In the sixteenth century, a professor of theology named Martin Luther objected to the selling of indulgences, or freedom from punishment for sins, by the Roman Catholic Church. His objections sparked the Reformation, a movement to fix problems in the Roman Catholic Church, and the

? Did You Know?

In A.D. 786, Charlemagne defeated the armies of Lombardy and became the protector of the papal state in Rome. He was crowned kaiser, or king, in A.D. 800 by a grateful pope, whose armies had been near defeat.

◀ A detail of the shrine of Charlemagne, which is located in the Palatine Chapel in the German city of Aachen.

beginning of a new Protestant Church. The Reformation led to a split within the states of the Holy Roman Empire. By 1555, it was up to the prince of each state in the area that is now Germany to choose his state's main religion.

THE THIRTY YEARS' WAR

From 1618 to 1648, the Holy Roman Empire was ravaged by the Thirty Years' War. Protestant and Catholic states fought with one another over their religious differences. The conflict was so long and bloody that, by the time the war ended in 1648, Germany was devastated. The Empire took one hundred years to recover from the effects of the Thirty Years' War, and many of the smaller states struggled to survive. Larger states, such as Prussia, managed to grow and develop, but this process was overtaken by the invasion of the

 Bavarian Protestants attending church. On special occasions, many German people wear traditional clothing to show their strong links to the local area.

French. In 1806, Napoleon Bonaparte, the emperor of France, defeated local armies and ended the Holy Roman Empire. In 1815, following Napoleon's defeat by a coalition of British, Russian, and Prussian armies, Germany was reorganized into a confederation of thirty-five states, all of which were fiercely independent.

? Did You Know?

Between 1348 and 1350, the Black Death, an epidemic of the bubonic plague, killed one out of every four people in Germany.

In the 1830s, the Industrial Revolution came to Germany. Mines were excavated, engineering and steel works were opened, and new railroad lines were built. With its military might and its plentiful natural resources, Prussia became one of the strongest states in the German Confederation. In 1871, Otto von Bismarck became Prussia's chancellor, and he was eager to unite Germany under Prussian rule.

BIZMARCK

With skillful diplomacy, Bismarck managed to unite Germany in 1871, with Berlin as its capital. The national colors were established as black, red, and white (later gold). Germany began a process of rapid industrialization. By 1890, Germany had established important coal, steel, engineering, electrical, and chemical industries. The country also began to build up a powerful army and navy.

WORLD WAR I

In 1914, the assassination of Franz Ferdinand, archduke of Austria, in Sarajevo, triggered the start of World War I. In this war, Germany, Austria, and Turkey (the Central Powers) joined together against Britain, France, and Russia (the Allied Powers). In 1917, the United States entered the war on the side of the Allies, who triumphed over the Central Powers in 1918. Following defeat in World War I, Germany was politically and economically weak. This situation contributed to the growth of extremist groups like the Nazi Party.

▼ The stadium built by the Nazis in Berlin for the 1936 Olympic games. During the 1936 Olympics, Hitler and his supporters tried—and failed—to convince the world of the supremacy of their ideas.

THE NAZI ERA

During the 1930s, German nationalism became a major force in uniting the country and led to the rise of the Nazi party. In 1933, Nazi leader Adolf Hitler came to power. Under Hitler's dictatorial rule, Germany built new roads and encouraged the rapid growth of industries linked with the armed forces, especially shipbuilding, aircraft manufacturing, and chemical making. Another important part of Hitler's plan for restoring Germany as a world power was the promoting of the belief that the Germans were a superior "Aryan" race. The Nazis blamed Jews and other minority groups for Germany's economic and social problems. They organized boycotts of Jewish-owned businesses and expelled Jews from jobs in teaching, medicine, and other public services.

By 1939, Germany was prosperous and had rebuilt its armed forces. Hitler saw his chance to expand German territory for Aryan occupation. In September 1939, the Nazis invaded Poland—beginning World War II— and, as a result, Britain and France declared war on Germany. In 1941, the United States and the Soviet Union joined with Britain and France. These countries defeated Germany in 1945, and British, American, French, and Soviet troops occupied the country.

During World War II, the Nazis had begun a systematic attempt to kill all Jews in the parts of Europe they conquered. They put the Jews in concentration camps, many of which provided slave labor for large factories. Most of these camps were in Eastern Europe, and some of them had gas chambers in which it is estimated that six million Jews were murdered in what is known as the Holocaust.

 Did You Know?

On February 13, 1945, Allied aircraft bombed and destroyed most of the ancient German city of Dresden. Parts of Dresden were later rebuilt according to its old pattern.

Focus on: Concentration Camps

During World War II, the Nazis used concentration camps to detain and kill millions of Jews, as well as political opponents, homosexuals, gypsies, disabled people, and resistance fighters. There were twenty-two Nazi camps. In camps such as Auschwitz, Belsen, Sobibor, and Treblinka, inmates were gassed, shot, beaten, or tortured to death. Seven million people were sent to these camps, but only half a million of them survived. Many concentration camps have been preserved and are now open to the public to remind people of the atrocities committed in them and to help ensure that they never happen again.

▲ Visitors to Dachau, a concentration camp, learn about the terrible crimes that took place there.

After 1945, disputes between the Allies and the Soviet Union led to the establishment of two separate countries in Germany. West Germany, or the Federal Republic of Germany, was supported by the United States and the Western allies. East Germany, or the German Democratic Republic, was supported by the Soviet Union and its communist allies. Bonn became the capital of West Germany, and East Berlin became the capital of East Germany.

GERMANY: EAST AND WEST

East Germany became a communist country. Its secret police, the Stasi, were hated for the control they exerted over people's lives. The Stasi encouraged family members to spy and inform on one another. East German farms

▼ Between 1961 and 1989, the Brandenburg Gate in Berlin, shown here lit up at night, was the dividing line between East and West Germany.

were collectivized, or organized into large, government-owned units. Industry was also tightly controlled by the government, which set targets for industry, agriculture, and all aspects of life. In agriculture, the government's goal was to make the country independent. Economic growth in East Germany, however, was slow because of a lack of natural resources, poor organization, and insufficient finances for investment.

In contrast, West Germany and other Western European countries received economic aid from the United States to help them recover from World War II. West Germany, therefore, enjoyed rapid economic growth. West Germany's economic success brought a flood of refugees from East Germany. In 1961, to prevent further loss of its population, East Germany built a wall dividing East Berlin and West Berlin. In the fall of 1989, however, mass

▲ A memorial to the East Germans shot or arrested trying to flee to the West stands at Checkpoint Charlie, a crossing point in the Berlin Wall.

AFTER 1990

In 1990, the process of reunifying Germany began in earnest. The West German chancellor, Helmut Kohl, was the driving force behind the privatization of industry in the eastern regions and the reinstatement of Berlin as Germany's capital city. During the 1990s, Germany rebuilt many of the railroads, roads, and factories in the eastern regions that had been so neglected over the previous twenty years. In 1999, Germany joined the European Monetary Union, and the country promoted the idea of creating a common currency. On January 1, 2002, the first euro notes and coins began to circulate.

In 1992, Germany, along with other NATO countries, took part in the invasion of Bosnia, to restore peace to a region plagued by civil strife. When coalition forces from the United States and Britain invaded Iraq in 2003 to overthrow Saddam Hussein, however, Germany spoke out against the move. Since then, Germany has campaigned for the withdrawal of troops from Iraq as soon as possible. Germany is also one of the nations involved in the campaign to write off the debt of the world's eighteen poorest nations.

demonstrations by groups opposed to communist rule took place in East Germany, and the end of a divided Germany swiftly followed. The Berlin Wall was torn down, and in November 1989, the frontier between East Germany and West Germany was opened. In August 1990, a Unification Treaty was signed between East and West Germany.

 Did You Know?

In 1948, the Soviet Union blockaded West Berlin for nearly a year during the Cold War, the conflict of ideas between the United States and it allies and the Soviet Union and its allies. During the blockade, Western powers organized 300,000 flights to airlift food and fuel into West Berlin.

CHAPTER 3

Landscape and Climate

Germany has many different landscapes, from broad plains to high mountains and deep valleys. The landscape of the north and northeast of the country tends to be flat, rising in height toward the Alpine mountains of the south. Most of Germany's rivers, such as the Elbe and the Rhine, flow north or northwest, following the relief of the land. They drain into the Baltic or the North Sea. The exception is the Danube, which flows east into Austria. The Rhine is the most important river in the country because it is so long and because it is navigable by barges for much of its length. It rises in the Swiss Alps and flows for 820 miles (1,319 km) to the Netherlands, where it drains into the North Sea. The Rhine forms part of Germany's frontier with France.

THE EUROPEAN PLAIN

The North Sea coast of Germany is flat. In this area, the shallow sea freezes in most winters. Sandy beaches and sand spits are found along this part of the coast. Further east are German-owned islands in the Baltic, of which the largest is Rügen, which is famous for its chalk cliffs. Most of northern Germany is part of the European Plain, a section of land that extends from France to Russia. This area consists of low plains, shallow lakes, and marshes.

▼ Germany's Baltic coast consists of long, sandy beaches flanked by low, chalk hills. In spite of the cold winds and cool sea, it is a favorite vacation destination for many Germans.

THE CENTRAL UPLANDS

To the south are the Central Uplands. This area includes the Eifel, with its famous lakes that fill the craters of extinct volcanoes, and the valleys of the rivers Moselle and Rhine. The Rhine cuts through the Central Uplands to form a gorge where picturesque castles are perched on clifftops overlooking the rivers. Vines grow on the warm valley slopes, and their grapes are used to make world famous wines.

▲ Castles like this were built above the Rhine to protect local people and to extract tolls from vessels using the river.

 Did You Know?

The lowest point in Germany is 11.6 feet (3.5 meter) below sea level near the Baltic coast. The country's highest point is the 9,721-foot (2,963-m) Zugspitze Mountain in the Alps.

Focus on: Flooding

With so many major rivers, large parts of Germany are affected by flooding. Floods in Germany usually happen during spring, when the mountain snows melt, or in fall, when heavy rains swell the rivers. In 1997, the Oder River in eastern Germany burst its banks and flooded the surrounding farmland and towns. In 2002, the Elbe River rose from its normal summer level of 6 feet 6 inches (2 m) to 30 feet 2 inches (9.2 m), a new record high, and overflowed on to the surrounding flood plain. Buildings in Dresden were flooded and twelve thousand people had to be evacuated from their homes. The mayor of Dresden estimated that it would cost hundreds of millions of euros to repair the damage. As the tide of floodwater swept further downriver, another eight thousand people had to be evacuated from the town of Torgau.

THE ALPS

South of the Central Uplands are the Alps. The Alps are high rugged mountains that rise to over 6,562 feet (2,000 m), some of which are covered with snow and ice in winter. The lower slopes of the Alps are thickly wooded. Areas such as Bavaria's Black Forest give way on the lowest slopes to meadows. Blue gentians and other wild flowers used to be found in these meadows, but the use of chemicals in farming has reduced their numbers.

INFLUENCES ON THE CLIMATE

Germany's location in central Europe is where the warm, wet winds from the west meet the cold, dry winds from the east. As a result, weather in Germany can vary widely. In a severe winter, temperatures may fall well below freezing and stay there for several weeks, especially if the land is covered with snow and there is a persistent high-pressure system over central Europe. The following year, the winter may be mild and wet with relatively little snow. Weather conditions in Germany also vary from region to region. On average, the western areas have milder winters

(32 °Fahrenheit/0 °Celsius) and cooler summers (62 °F/15 °C) than the eastern regions, which have cold winters (23 °F/-4 °C) and hot, sunny summers (72 °F/20 °C).

The climate of northern and western Germany is affected by the moderating influence of the sea, which causes milder winters and cooler summers than in areas further east. Winters in the east may be so cold that the rivers, lakes, and seas freeze for several weeks. The central and eastern parts of the country have a shorter growing season and more days of frost. For example, Aachen has only forty-two days of frost per year while Berlin has ninety days. Altitude also affects temperatures, which fall by about 1.8 °F (1 °C) for every 492 feet (150 meters) of altitude. This is called the lapse rate. For example, the plateau of the Rhine River is 5.4 °F (3 °C) to 7.2 °F (4 °C) colder than the

▼ On the rich, volcanic soils of western Germany, vines are grown in straight rows to make it easier for farmers to prune and care for the plants and pick the grapes.

nearby city of Cologne, which is around 262
feet (80 m) lower. The area around Freiburg
in southwest Germany is known for being the
sunniest place in the country.

Germany receives between 23.5 and 31.5 inches
(60–80 centimeters) of rain and snow per year,
but this amount varies from place to place.
High areas, such as the Black Forest and the
Harz Mountains, receive more than 47 inches
(119 cm) per year. The driest places in the
country are in the south and east, where the
Alps protect the land from rain-bearing winds.

There is heavy winter snowfall in the Alps in
the south. When this snow melts in spring, it
often causes the flooding of rivers such as the
Rhine and the Danube.

▼ The Alps in Germany are high enough to retain
snow well into the spring, making them attractive
areas for late-season skiing.

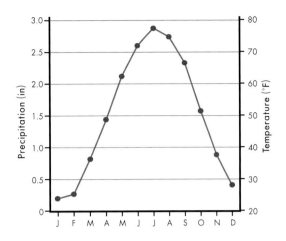

▲ Average monthly climate conditions in Berlin

 Did You Know?
In May of each year, some parts of central
Germany have a brief cool spell that is called
"the three ice saints." Each spring, a warm, dry
wind known as the *Fohn* blows in southern
Germany. The Fohn can melt several feet of
snow within a few hours.

CHAPTER 4

Population and Settlements

Germany has a total population of 82.5 million. Of this total, about 15 million live in the region that formerly comprised East Germany, an area that is still less densely populated than the west. Most Germans live in villages and small towns; even the largest cities are modest in size compared with other world cities. About 27 million people live in cities with more than 100,000 inhabitants, 49 million live in small towns of between 2,000 and 100,000 people, and the rest live in the countryside.

POPULATION DENSITY

The most densely populated regions in Germany are Greater Berlin; the Ruhr industrial area, near the border with the Netherlands; and the areas around Frankfurt-am-Main, Wiesbaden, and Mannheim. Germany has only nineteen cities with more than 300,000 people, of which only two—Berlin and Frankfurt-am-Main—are in the former East Germany. Germany's most populated cities are Berlin (3.3 million people), Hamburg (2.7 million), and Stuttgart (2.7 million).

Following reunification in 1990, the population of Berlin was expected to grow rapidly to reach 8 million by 2010. Many young families, however, have left Berlin since 1990 in search of a better quality of life in villages and small towns in the countryside. It is now thought that the population of Berlin will remain at its present size for the foreseeable future. In Germany as a whole, many people are leaving

▼ In some ways, Germany's financial center, Frankfurt-am-Main, looks like a typical modern city with office blocks and skyscrapers. But many of its buildings—including its old Jewish quarter—date back several centuries.

 Even relatively small German villages have areas for recreational sports. These facilities are part of a drive to improve the health of young people.

large towns and cities for the cleaner, healthier environment of the countryside. City dwellers are buying up farms and cottages close to towns. Often they then sell off the land and redesign the buildings. During the day, these villages are very quiet because everyone is away at work. The villages only come to life in the evenings, when people return to their homes.

POPULATION GROWTH

Germany has about nine births and ten deaths for each one thousand people in the country. The population would be shrinking were it not for some small-scale immigration. Even with this immigration, overall population growth is only 0.1 percent.

Germany has an aging population. About 15 percent of the population is 14 years old or younger, 68 percent is between 15 and 64 years old, and 17 percent is over 65. Because in the future there will be relatively few younger people to support many older people, this high percentage of older people is causing serious concern.

Population Data

- Population: 82.5 million
- Population 0–14 yrs: 15%
- Population 15–64 yrs: 68%
- Population 65+ yrs: 17%
- Population growth rate: 0.1%
- Population density: 611.9 per sq mile/ 236.2 per sq km
- Urban population: 88%
- Major cities: Berlin 3,328,000
              Hamburg 2,686,000
              Stuttgart 2,705,000

Source: United Nations and World Bank

? Did You Know?

Between 1945 and 1990, ten million people fled from East Germany to West Germany.

One problem is the question of who will pay for the health care, nursing homes, pensions, and other requirements of an older population. A range of solutions to the aging-population problem has been proposed, among them tax cuts to encourage people to have larger families and relaxed immigration laws to allow people from abroad to live and work in Germany.

work doing the more menial jobs that Germans did not want, such as bus driving and garbage disposal. Guest workers became permanent residents of Germany but not citizens. In many cases, whole families moved to Germany. By 1973, there were 2.3 million guest workers in the country, and by 2004, the number had grown to 3.2 million.

In the 1970s, economic recession ended the process of immigration, but most guest workers remained in Germany. Today, these immigrants form an important part of German society and are counted in the census. The Turkish ethnic community consists of more than two million people, while the Serbian (Yugoslav) community has 715,000 people. Germany has also become a center for asylum seekers who come from countries such as the former Yugoslavia or from other central European countries, such

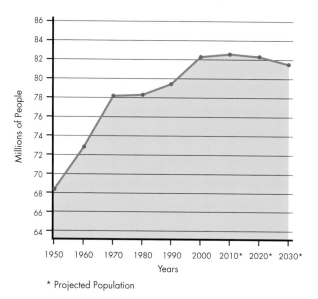

* Projected Population

▲ Population growth, 1950–2030

GUEST WORKERS

Germany has become home to many different ethnic groups. In the nineteenth century, Polish miners came to Germany for work. More recently, the very rapid economic growth in the 1950s and 1960s meant that immigrants were needed to provide labor for German industry. The German government encouraged guest workers, called *Gastarbeiter*, to come to Germany from countries such as Turkey, Morocco, and Yugoslavia. A guest worker is someone who moves to a country to live and work for more than one year. These workers came to Germany to find better paid jobs and a better quality of life than were available in their own countries. Many of them found

 Did You Know?

Since 1990, 2.5 million people from Kazakhastan and other parts of eastern Europe have settled in Germany and have been allowed to become citizens.

▼ These musicians from Turkey earn a living by playing for passersby in Frankfurt.

as Albania. The asylum seekers must undergo a strict application process before they are allowed to stay in Germany, and some are either sent back to their country of origin or deported to another country.

? Did You Know?

Only about 12.5% of people who seek asylum in Germany are allowed to stay in the country.

▼ A mosque in Usingen that was built to serve the members of the local Muslim community was damaged by fire. The fire might have been accidental or it might have been the result of a racist arson attack.

Focus on: Citizenship

In 1999, a law was passed to update Germany's citizenship laws. The old laws dated back to 1913, and they defined nationality according to blood not birthplace. According to these laws, the children of guest workers could not become German citizens and, therefore, could not vote in elections. Beginning in 2000, anyone born to non-German parents is given "provisional citizenship." At the age of twenty-three, they must decide whether to retain the nationality of their parents or to become full German citizens.

CHAPTER 5

Government and Politics

Germany is a constitutional democracy with a federal system of government. The country's head of state is the federal president, who has little political power but represents the country on national matters. The federal president is elected to a five-year term and can only be re-elected once. The chancellor holds the real power. He or she appoints ministers to the government and, with them, runs the key elements of government such as health care, education, and defense.

The country is divided into sixteen states, or *Länder*. The people of each Länder have strong feelings about retaining their own independence and identity. For example, many people in Bavaria refer to themselves as Bavarians first and Germans second. Each Länder has considerable power over its own affairs.

THE GERMAN PARLIAMENT

Since 1999, Germany's parliament has met in the imposing Reichstag building in Berlin. The country's parliament has two main houses: the Bundestag and the Bundesrat. Together, they form Germany's legislature. A majority is needed for most laws to be passed. A two-thirds majority in both houses is needed to make changes to the country's constitution.

▼ This special session of the German Bundestag was convened in 2002 to hear an address by U.S. president George Bush (center, standing at podium).

The Bundestag elects the chancellor and initiates most of the country's legislation. About half the Bundestag consists of representatives elected directly in the Länder. The other half is made up of delegates appointed by political parties. The reason that not all of the Bundestag members are elected is to prevent local issues from dominating the political agenda. For a party to be allowed to appoint members to the Bundestag, it must win 5 percent of the vote at a national election or have three elected MPs.

The Bundesrat is the upper house of the German parliament. Its members are made up of delegates who represent the sixteen Länder. They are appointed by parliament.

ELECTIONS

Elections are held every four years, and the chancellor can only be replaced if there is a new candidate for the post with an assured majority.

 The seat of the German Bundestag is the Reichstag. One of the building's main features is the glistening glass dome that covers its plenary hall.

Did You Know?

In Germany, October 3 is National Unity Day. On this day, Germans celebrate the political and cultural coming together of the German people.

In practice, the chancellor is the leader of the party that wins most of the votes in the election. Voting is not compulsory, but turnout is usually about 80 percent. This voter turnout is much higher than in most other countries of western Europe. Germans realize the importance of voting and see it as part of their civic duty. German women have had the vote since 1918 and are well represented in German politics. In 2004, they made up 26 percent of the Bundestag. The chief political parties in Germany are the Christian Democratic Union (CDU), also known as the Christian Democrat Party (CDP); the Social Democratic Party (SPD); the Green Party (Alliance 90/The Greens); and the Free Democratic Party (FDP).

ISSUES EMERGING FROM REUNIFICATION

Although Germany was officially reunified in 1990, the real work of bringing East and West Germany together took some time. Helmut Kohl, the German chancellor and head of the CDP, drove the process. He oversaw huge changes, especially in the former East Germany, where industries were privatized and modernized. Kohl reassured the people in neighboring states, such as Poland, who were worried about the growing political and economic power of the new Germany. Kohl also was the driving force behind the move of the country's parliament from Bonn back to Berlin.

During the 1990s, the role of women began to change in the former East Germany. Before reunification, about 90 percent of East German women were employed or in training programs. This was because there was a serious labor shortage caused by the flight of many young men to West Germany. After reunification, however, about 63 percent of these women were out of work as a result of the closure of factories and offices that could not compete with the larger and more efficient firms from the West. Some of these women have found work in offices and shops, but in 2003, 42 percent of the

▼ The city of Dresden was very badly damaged by Allied bombing during World War II. Since 1990, it has been carefully rebuilt using the original plans.

total female labor force was still out of work in the former East Germany.

Since reunification, Germany's government has established programs throughout the country to help women, especially those with young children, return to work. In 2002, opinion polls suggested that 13 percent of employed women in the country's eastern areas and 14 percent of employed women in the country's western areas placed more importance on their careers than on having a family. Women in the east and the west, however, differed in their attitudes toward training to gain new skills or other forms of personal development. In the east, women sought self-development mainly to earn more money and achieve a higher standard of living. In the west, women pursued it more for reasons of personal fulfillment.

One of the most difficult issues to emerge from reunification was that of abortion. In East Germany, abortion had been legal for up to twelve weeks after conception. Laws in West Germany were different. After 1995, abortion was declared illegal in the newly reunified Germany. It was not, however, considered a criminal act if carried out within twelve weeks after conception and with compulsory counseling, and exceptions to the law were made for medical reasons.

Focus on: The Green Party

Germany's Green Party (Alliance 90/The Greens) was founded in the 1970s. The Greens won their first seat in the state parliament of Bremen in 1979. The party's membership grew in the 1980s when the Greens became part of the movement that supported world peace and increased ecological awareness. In 1993, the party joined forces with Alliance 90, a confederation of civil rights groups from the former East Germany. The high point for the Greens was 1998, when they won forty-seven seats and formed a coalition government with the SPD. Since 1998, the Greens have had a less powerful voice in government, but they have still been able to make a deal with the energy industry to phase out nuclear power by 2030 and replace it with renewable energy.

▶ **This member of Germany's Green party travels to and from the Reichstag by bicycle in order to demonstrate the use of nonpolluting transportation.**

CHAPTER 6

Energy and Resources

Germany's industrial growth has been fueled by energy generated from fossil fuels such as coal, oil, and natural gas. Germany used to be rich in both black coal and brown coal. Brown coal, which is called lignite, has less energy value than black coal and creates a lot of air pollution. The main black coalfield in Germany is the Ruhr, in the western part of the country. Since the 1890s, the Ruhr has provided energy for Germany's rapidly growing industries. Coal is still produced there but in much smaller quantities than in the past. This is because, in the last thirty years or so, mines have become unprofitable and have closed down. Brown coal is still used to generate electricity in Germany's eastern regions, but it is more valuable as a raw material for the chemical industry than as a fuel.

NATURAL GAS

Fossil fuels are used to generate 62 percent of all electricity in Germany. Most of this electricity, however, is generated not by burning coal but by burning natural gas. Natural gas is the fuel of choice because it is cleaner than coal and does not contribute to acid rain in the same way. Germany produces small amounts of natural gas and oil in the northwestern areas, but most of the country's supply of these fuels is imported from Russia via long pipelines.

▼ A modern coal mine in the Saarland area of Germany. The coal seams mined today are deeper and more fractured than those mined in the past, so mines have been modernized. Mechanized coal-cutting equipment is used to keep costs down.

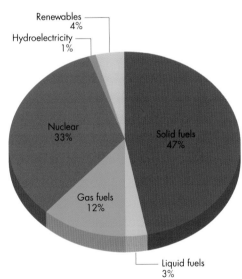

▲ Wind farms like this one are becoming a familiar sight in parts of Germany. They make a valuable contribution to generating electricity in a way that does not cause pollution.

▲ Energy generation by source

Focus on: Hydroelectric Power

Hydroelectric power (HEP) provides 1 percent of Germany's electricity. Some of Germany's HEP stations are located along the fast-flowing rivers found in the Alpine areas of the southern part of the country. In these areas, the mountains provide the steep gradients necessary for HEP generation. A few other HEP stations have been built along the major rivers in Germany, such as the Rhine and the Elbe. Hydroelectric power stations are expensive to build but cheap to run because the fuel—water—is free. HEP is also popular because it causes little or no pollution, unlike most other ways of generating power.

 Did You Know?

Germany has nineteen nuclear power stations. In the 1990s, antinuclear protests were widespread, and trains carrying nuclear waste were threatened by angry protesters. Twenty-thousand police officers were employed to protect these trains from attack.

NUCLEAR POWER

Nuclear power provides 33 percent of Germany's electricity. The country began building nuclear power stations during the 1970s, when it seemed that there might be a shortage of coal or oil in the future. Nuclear power stations have been very controversial in Germany because of the danger of radiation leaks. Use of nuclear power also brings the problem of how to safely dispose of the radioactive waste it generates.

Germany's nuclear waste is currently stored on the sites of its nuclear power plants. Safe, long-term storage for the country's nuclear waste remains a huge problem. The phasing out of nuclear power only partly solves the problem because it leaves the issue of how to dispose of the existing waste. The first nuclear power station to be eliminated in Germany closed down in 2004.

RENEWABLE ENERGY

The remaining 4 percent of Germany's energy is derived from wind and solar power. The government is eager to increase electricity generation by renewable sources such as these to 10 percent by 2020. Wind energy is an important alternative source of electricity generation in Germany. Modern wind turbines have very large rotors of 197 feet (60 m), and their blades can spin at up to 250 miles per hour (400 kph). Wind turbines are usually built in clusters called wind farms. In Germany, wind farms are located mostly along the Baltic and North Sea coasts, and there are plans to construct some offshore wind farms. People who live near the farms have criticized them because of their noise and appearance, but wind farms cause no air pollution and do not contribute to acid rain or global warming.

▲ These houses in Heidelberg have solar panels on their roofs that heat their hot water systems.

SOLAR POWER

Solar power is generated by the Sun's rays falling on to silicon cells, which generate electricity. Solar cells are arranged in panels, which are usually located on the roofs of buildings. In Germany, a program aims to install solar panels in one million homes by 2010. The use of solar energy on a large scale, however, tends to be very expensive. Solar cells are not very efficient, so research into improving them continues, but they clearly have a future in the sunniest parts of Germany, such as Freiburg, in the southwest.

OTHER RESOURCES

In the past, much of Germany was densely forested, but over the years, large areas of trees have been felled to provide fuel and timber. This occurred on a large scale in the eighteenth century, when the glass-making industry needed timber to make the charcoal that was used to heat sand and convert it to glass. The cleared areas were replanted with fast-growing conifers. This replanting changed some deciduous woodland areas, such as the Harz Mountains, into coniferous forests. In spite of these changes, Germany still has large areas of deciduous woodland, such as parts of the Black Forest, that are home to wood carving and timber industries.

Another resource is fish. Fishing fleets operate along the North and Baltic Sea coasts of Germany, but they have been cut back in recent years as part of an attempt to conserve fish stocks, especially in the North Sea.

Germany used to be rich in minerals such as iron ore, sulphur, lead, and zinc. Few of these minerals are still mined in Germany, because it is very expensive to extract the deposits from the great depths at which they are found.

Energy Data

- Energy consumption as % of world total: 3.6
- Energy consumption by sector (% of total),
  Industry: 34
  Transportation: 28
  Agriculture: 1
  Services: 10
  Residential: 27
- CO_2 emissions as % of world total: 3.5
- CO_2 emissions per capita in tons per year: 11

Source: World Resources Institute

 Did You Know?

In Germany, over one million trees are cut down each year to make timber and wood pulp.

▼ Germany spends over $12 million per year on timber imports from the rest of the world. Timber harvested from the Black Forest, such as that shown below, reduces the need for imports.

CHAPTER 7

Economy and Income

Agriculture is one of Germany's smallest—but one of its most important—industries. Although it accounts for only 2.8 percent of employment and 1 percent of the Gross National Income (GNI), agriculture is central to the country's economy. This is because Germany produces 53 percent of its own food on highly efficient farms. The country still has many farms of fewer than 25 acres (10 hectares) that are worked by part-time farmers who usually have another job in addition to farming. Some large farms are run to gain the maximum return for the input of time, money, and expertise of the farmers. About 60 percent of Germany's farmers, however, have second jobs. Between 1950 and 2002, the number of farms in Germany decreased from 2.1 million to 666,000.

FARM ANIMALS

Dairy farming—the production of milk, butter, and cheese—is well suited to the cool conditions found throughout most of Germany. In the drier areas, wheat, barley, and sugar beets are grown. In the warmer southern parts of the country, maize is grown as feed for cattle and pigs. Most pigs in Germany are reared in livestock units, which consist of large sheds with huge grain silos next to them. The silos provide the feed for the pigs used to meet German people's demand for sausage (*Wurst*).

Economic Data

📁 Gross National Income (GNI) in U.S.$: 2,084,631,000,000
📁 World rank by GNI: 3
📁 GNI per capita in U.S.$: 25,250
📁 World rank by GNI per capita: 22
📁 Economic growth: 0%
Source: World Bank

 Did You Know?

Germany has over 22 million pigs, 19 million cattle, and 1.2 million sheep. Pork is the most popular meat among the German people, followed by veal, chicken, and beef.

▼ Since reunification, the mechanization of farming in the eastern parts of Germany has resulted in greater efficiency and higher crop yields.

▲Ripe grapes are picked from the vines and loaded into trucks before being made into wine.

WINE PRODUCTION

Germany is an important producer and exporter of wine. Most of the country's vineyards are on south-facing slopes along the valley of the Rhine and its tributaries. Over the years, the steep hillsides have been terraced to provide level ground on which vines can be grown. To help consumers tell one type of wine from the other, Rhine wine is sold in brown bottles and wine from the Moselle area is sold in green bottles. Germany is also a major producer of beer. Barley and hops are grown throughout the county and are used to produce high-quality beers.

COOPERATIVES IN THE EAST

Prior to reunification, the eastern areas of Germany were cultivated by large farming cooperatives controlled by the government. The government told farmers what to grow, when to plow, and when to plant. This system was very inefficient because it lacked adequate resources, such as tractors and combine harvesters, to work the land. Little incentive existed for people to work hard because they did not own the land and did not stand to benefit directly if production increased. After 1990, the cooperative farms were broken up or sold to groups of farmers. These farmers are now free to make their own decisions about what to grow and where and when to grow it.

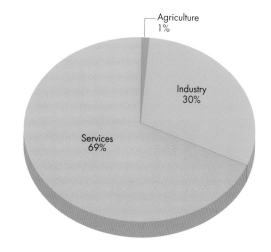

▲ Contribution by sector to national income

ENGINEERING AND MANUFACTURING

Germany is one of the world's biggest economies. German engineers have a reputation for designing high-quality products, and German industry produces high-tech goods such as cameras, lenses, and cars. Among the best-known German brands are Mercedes, BMW, Volkswagen, Zeiss, and Bosch. Manufacturing industries employ about 33 percent of the German workforce—about two million people—mainly in medium-sized companies with fewer than one hundred employees. Germany's manufacturers produce a range of consumer goods such as television sets, computers, washing machines, refrigerators, and microwave ovens.

Heavy industries producing cars, vans, trucks, ships, and a wide range of machinery are still important in Germany. Many of the goods they produce are exported all over the world.

▼ The Mercedes car factory is one of the largest and most modern in the world. Many Mercedes buyers from Europe travel to the factory to pick up their new car and take a tour of the factory.

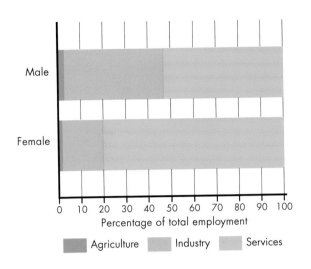

▲ Labor force by sector and gender

 Did You Know?

The original Volkswagen Beetle was developed in the 1930s, during the regime of Adolf Hitler. The original model stayed in production until the 1980s, when it was replaced by a new design of Beetle.

Focus on: Eastern Germany

By 1989, over 80 percent of the workforce in East Germany worked in state controlled industries. After reunification, it became clear that aging equipment, overstaffing, and inefficiency were hampering industry in the east. After 1990, many industries in eastern Germany were put up for sale, but firms in western Germany were reluctant to invest in them, so many of them were sold to former East German managers. New machinery was introduced and factories were re-equipped, but the cost of this has been high. The east is still only 70 percent as roductive as the west.

CHEMICAL INDUSTRY

The German chemical industry first developed on the brown coalfields because these fields supplied the raw material for the industry. Soon, however, oil became the new raw material of the industry. Chemical factories were built along the Rhine and the Elbe and oil was imported to them by barge or pipeline. The chemical industry is very important to the Germany economy, and it produces everything from pharmaceuticals to plastics and paint.

ENVIRONMENTAL PROTECTION

Almost one million people in Germany work in industries connected with environmental protection—as many as work in the car industry. Germany has 18 percent of the world market in this field. Much of the country's environmental work concerns the manage-ment of waste, which is a fast growing sector of the economy. Germany is a leading producer of vehicles for collecting waste, including green waste, paper, glass, and textiles—for recycling. Germany also produces most of the equipment used to measure the amounts of pollutants in air and water and to monitor traffic flow in major cities.

SERVICE INDUSTRIES

Over 63 percent of Germany's workforce is involved in service industries such as transportation, retailing, finance, and professional and public services. Some of the people employed in service industries work in offices, many of which are located in large buildings. The skylines of modern cities, such as Berlin and Frankfurt, are dominated by these office buildings, which are usually located close to city center shops. This concentration of offices leads to traffic congestion, so some new office parks have been built on the edges of cities to provide office employment away from city centers. Some other offices are based in modest buildings in the older parts of towns and cities. The tourist industry is another part of the service sector, employing people who arrange winter sports vacations, city vacations, and vacations in the lakes and mountains.

 Did You Know?

Although Berlin is the capital of Germany, only eleven of the five hundred largest corporations are based in Berlin, with fifty in Hamburg and another thirty-three in Munich.

▲ Planners in cities such as Berlin try to make sure that modern chemical factories like this one have trees planted around them to reduce their impact on the landscape.

CHAPTER 8

Global Connections

Germany is an important member of the European Union (EU), an alliance of twenty-five European countries. In 1957, six countries, including Germany and France, formed the European Economic Community (EEC), the forerunner of the EU. This alliance between France and Germany was, in part, an attempt to move away from the conflicts of the past and establish a new, positive relationship at the heart of Europe.

PROMOTING TRADE

An early aim of the EEC was to promote trade between its members. Because it was very successful in doing this, other countries joined the EEC, and the group's interests expanded

beyond trade to include social and judicial cooperation. In 1993, the EEC's name was changed to European Union to reflect its wider concerns. Since 1993, the EU has become a much broader organization, with a parliament elected by the member countries and a

> **? Did You Know?**
>
> The city of Strasbourg is half in Germany and half in France. For this reason, it was chosen as the location for the headquarters of the EU.

▼ This photo shows a branch of the headquarters of the European Union located in Strasbourg. The other branch is in Brussels, Belgium.

president and commissioners who are responsible for its day-to-day running. Germany occupies a central position in Europe and has a long history of contacts with eastern Europe. The country works to foster trade and investment in eastern Europe, and it was influential in encouraging eastern European countries such as the Czech Republic, Slovenia, and Poland to become members of the EU. These countries joined the EU in May 2004, together with nine other nations.

▲ The European Central Bank is located in Frankfurt, Germany. The statue outside the bank is of the symbol of the euro, the EU's common currency.

NATO

Germany is also a key member of the North Atlantic Treaty Organization (NATO). This group was formed at the end of World War II to help defend western Europe against the spread of communism from the Soviet Union during the Cold War, the conflict of ideas between the Soviet Union (and its communist allies) and the West (the United States, Britain, and their allies). Following the collapse of the former Soviet Union in 1991, the threat from communism in eastern Europe decreased and the role of NATO changed. The countries in NATO now provide troops for NATO activities, such as peacekeeping in Bosnia and the former Yugoslavia. German troops are a vital part of these operations.

The strength of Germany's economy makes it important to European and world trade. About 60 percent of all Germany's trade is with other EU countries. Germany's main trading partner is France, followed by the United States, Britain, and Italy. Other trading partners include the Netherlands, Austria, and Belgium.

 Did You Know?

The European Central Bank controls the euro zone, or the number of countries in which the euro is the currency.

Focus on: The Single European Currency

In 1999, Germany became one of the twelve EU countries to form the European Monetary Union (EMU). In the EMU, members ceased using old currencies, such as Germany's deutsche mark, and adopted the euro as their only currency. In 2002, euro notes and coins entered circulation for the first time in these twelve countries. There was much opposition in Germany to abandoning the deutsche mark because the unit of currency had been very stable. However, because of the success of the euro, by 2004, most Germans were happy to have abandoned the deutsche mark.

LINKS WITH RUSSIA

Germany is particularly interested in developing trade links with Russia. Much of Germany's oil and natural gas comes from Russia via the Friendship Pipeline, which begins in Siberia, reaches Germany by flowing through Poland, and continues to France and Britain. In return, Russia is eager to gain access to the technological expertise that is typical of most German industry. In particular, Germany manufactures the high-quality valves and control equipment that Russia needs for the building of even longer pipelines to carry oil from its Siberian oilfields. Russia has such large reserves of oil and gas that it will play a major role in the future the world's energy supply. Germany is eager to work with Russia on the building of pipelines.

▼ A ship loaded with boxcars at a Hamburg dock. Transportation of goods in this way has led to the rapid growth of dock areas like this one.

EXPORTS AND IMPORTS

Germany's main exports are machinery, vehicles, chemicals, and metals. Goods such as steel, tires, and vehicle panels are imported into Germany so that more complex and valuable manufactured goods such as cars, cameras, and electrical equipment can be made in German factories. Many of these high-value goods are exported. Germany's main imports are machinery, vehicles, chemicals, foodstuffs, textiles, and metals. This pattern of imports and exports shows that Germany is an advanced economy that produces many consumer goods, by processing imported semi-finished goods and then re-exporting the finished goods.

LINKS WITH THE FAR EAST

Germany is eager to develop closer links with countries such as China and Japan. In the last ten years, China—with low production costs that are based on low wage rates—has emerged as a major manufacturing nation. German

companies have realized the importance of importing some manufactured goods from China and switching their own production to high-tech and more expensive products. At the same time, German firms are moving some of their manufacturing to China to gain access to the Chinese market and to take advantage of China's lower wages and looser environmental protection laws.

Germany is also an important country in terms of international finance. The Bourse, or the German stock exchange, handles thousands of transactions, selling and buying shares in companies from all over the world. The Bourse, which is located in Frankfurt, has grown so rapidly over the last few years that it now rivals London as the financial capital of Europe. Germany's banks are very important to the European and world banking systems and deal with accounts from all over the world.

Did You Know?

In 2002, Germany's exports were worth $608 billion, and its imports were worth $487.3 billion.

▲ A stock trader at the Bourse uses two phones at the same time to place orders.

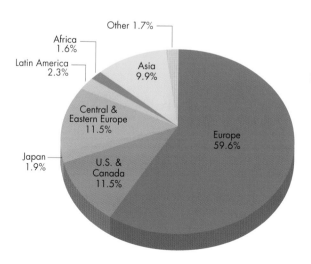

▲ Destination of exports by major trading region

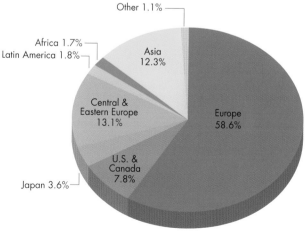

▲ Origin of imports by major trading region

CHAPTER 9

Transportation and Communications

Germany's superhighways, called *autobahnen*, are among the best in the world. The autobahnen were first built during the 1930s as a means of moving troops quickly and easily around the country. During World War II, many autobahnen were damaged, but they were rebuilt and extended in West Germany after 1945. In East Germany, the communist government did little to repair the autobahnen, but progress has been rapid since 1990. Other roads in Germany are also good and provide links with most parts of the country. New road-building projects continue, especially in the east, to connect the country's more remote areas with the rest of Germany.

▲ Germany has excellent superhighways. These roads are important because Germany's central position in Europe requires that most routes across Europe have to pass through the country.

TRANSPORTATION OF GOODS

An increasing number of goods are transported by road. These goods include even some heavy, bulky materials, such as steel and timber. The government is trying to prevent the worst effects of the rapid expansion of road transportation by recommending an integrated transportation system. This type of system involves moving goods by rail or water before transferring them to trucks to take them to their destination.

RAILROADS

German railroads, the *Deutsche Bahn*, operate a fast and frequent service between seven thousand main towns and cities. Germany is a big country, so its railroads are particularly important in connecting all the different areas. Since 1990, the network has been developed to integrate the eastern regions with the rest of the country. New high-speed links that cut travel times by up to 30 percent have been built to connect Berlin to cities such as Hanover and Munich. The railroads are also important in terms of the transportation of goods. Powerful new locomotives can carry larger loads over longer distances at greater speeds. Rail transportation is ideal for heavy, bulky materials such as chemicals, cars, and machinery. It is certain to play an important role within an integrated transportation system.

Some of Germany's major cities, such as Berlin, Frankfurt, Munich, and Hamburg, have underground rail systems. Berlin has two rail

systems: the older overground S-Bahn, which has been modernized, with thirteen lines, and the underground U-Bahn, which carries about 450,000 people each day on ten lines. These railway systems transport people to and from work and are valuable for reducing the volume of traffic in city centers. Germany also has a few privately run cog railways, on which trains run up some of the country's steepest mountains.

Transport & Communications Data

- Total roads: 143,286 miles/230,547 km
- Total paved roads: 143,286 miles/ 230,735 km
- Total unpaved roads: 0 miles/0 km
- Total railways: 28,608 miles/46,030 km
- Major airports: 550
- Cars per 1,000 people: 516
- Mobile phones per 1,000 people: 727
- Personal computers per 1,000 people: 431
- Internet users per 1,000 people: 412

Source: World Bank and CIA World Factbook

 Railroads are an important means of transportation in Germany. Many of the country's railroad lines have been electrified and modernized in an attempt to reduce travel times.

? Did You Know?

Germany has 28,608 miles (46,030 km) of railroad track, of which more than 13,000 miles (21,000 km) are electrified to allow faster speeds that enable Germany's railroads to compete with the airlines. The modern Inter City Express (ICE) trains travel at speeds of up to 174 miles per hour (280 kph).

AIR TRAVEL

Because of the size of the country and the relatively low cost of domestic flights, air travel within Germany is very popular. Most major cities have at least one airport. The main national airline is Lufthansa (although it is not owned by the government), which is based at Frankfurt. The country also has smaller airlines that offer services to other countries, to regional cities, and to the North Frisian Islands. Air travel is ideal for passengers who are in a hurry, and it is also good for shipping goods that are valuable but light, such as jewels, and for shipping perishable goods such as flowers and fruit. Berlin and Frankfurt have Germany's two main international airports.

▼ An airfield at Munich airport. The development of business travel and the growth of tourism, especially with the introduction of low cost airlines, has fueled the growth of air transportation in Germany.

WATER TRANSPORTATION

When speed of transportation is less important than cost, water transportation is often favored in Germany. Heavy, bulky goods such as coal, oil, iron ore, timber, and steel are usually transported by water, which is the best way of moving these goods cheaply and easily around the country. One of the largest industrial areas in the world has grown up along the Rhine in the Ruhr industrial zone around Duisburg. The industry in this area is based on local coal. Imported raw materials such as oil and iron ore are transported by water from Rotterdam to this area. Large barges use the rivers, especially the Rhine and the Elbe, to carry goods from ports such as Hamburg to the interior of the country. They also carry goods for export in the opposite direction. Smaller vessels carry tourists along rivers such as the Rhine, Moselle, and Elbe. In the summer, tourist steamers run on Lake Constance in southern Germany.

 A barge is used to transport a heavy, bulky load of coal on the Rhine.

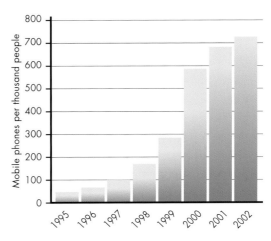

 Cellular phone use per 1,000 people , 1995–2002

TELECOMMUNICATIONS NETWORKS

Germany has one of the world's most advanced telecommunications systems. Huge amounts of money have been spent modernizing the tele-communications system in the former East Germany to bring it up to the standard of the rest of the country and to integrate the two systems. The country has an extensive system of telephone exchanges connected by modern networks of fiber-optic cable and also cellular telephone systems. These systems are growing rapidly and include links to many foreign countries.

With advances in technology, an increasing number of people in Germany are able to work at home and use the Internet to send their work into the office. This growing trend looks set to continue, with more than two hundred Internet service providers in Germany in 2004.

? Did You Know?

Germany has 77.8 million radios and 51.4 million television sets.

? Did You Know?

More than 89 percent of Germans under the age of fourteen have a cellular phone.

In Focus: Cars in Eastern Germany

Before reunification, cars were not widely used in East Germany because the state wanted to encourage people to use public transportation. Today, however, people in the eastern areas of Germany increasingly use cars to get to work, stores, and vacation and recreation destinations because they are relatively cheap to run, especially over short distances. The growing popularity of cars in eastern Germany, however, has created problems in towns and cities, including traffic jams, accidents, pollution, and a decline in the use of some forms of public transportation. Many cities have banned cars from their centers to improve the environment. Another problem with increasing car use is that groups such as the poor and single mothers, who may not have access to cars, are disadvantaged if the public transportation system is not adequate for their needs.

CHAPTER 10

Education and Health

Most children in Germany start school in *Kindergarten,* or nursery school, at the age of three. Germany was the first country to introduce schooling for young children, and different types of kindergartens are now offered around the world. Education is state funded and is compulsory for up to twelve or thirteen years beginning at the age of six. Germany has some religious and private schools, but most children go to public schools. Primary school lasts for four years and begins at the age of six.

▲ Germany was one of the first countries to appreciate that preschools give children a good start to their education.

SECONDARY EDUCATION

At the age of ten, children in Germany are divided into groups that attend different types of schools. Some go to a *Realschule*, or intermediate school; others go to the *Hauptschule*, or secondary school; and others go to a *Gesamtschule,* or comprehensive school. The most academically oriented children go to the *Gymnasium,* or grammar school. Each type of school offers general education and training, although the *Realschule* and *Hauptschule* concentrate on technical skills. School days start at 7:30 A.M. in summer and 8 A.M. in winter, and most children go home for lunch. During a mid-morning break of about thirty minutes, children are free to play and eat food they have brought from home. The school day ends between 2 P.M. and 3 P.M.

UNIVERSITIES

At the age of eighteen or nineteen, academically oriented students take the university entrance examination called the *Abitur*, a very rigorous test that may involve six one-hour exams. All university students must study at least one foreign language; English and French are the most popular choices. Students study for a diploma, a state examination, a master of arts, or a doctorate. Bachelor's level courses have also recently been introduced at many universities. The minimum period of study is four and one-half years, but it is usually closer to seven years. Slightly less than half of German university students are women. For young men, the combination of university education and military service makes most graduates at least twenty-eight years old before they start work.

? Did You Know?

Founded in 1386, the University of Heidelberg was the first university in Germany. Since then, it has grown in importance as a center of knowledge and research in all areas of science, arts, and medicine. It has thirty thousand students from eighty nations in eighteen faculties.

◀ The University of Heidelberg was founded in 1386 by Count Palatinate Ruprecht I.

COMPETITION FOR PLACES

Germany has 290 universities. They are mostly run by local states and funded in part by the federal government. Parents are legally required to support their children's education, and those who cannot afford to do so receive assistance from the federal government. There is a high demand for university places, which means that students have little choice of where they will study. A central board allocates university places, and students may then swap places among themselves. Swapping, however, is not possible in some subjects, such as medicine, for which there is a high demand for places. German university students are eager to study subjects such as engineering, history, business, and literature, but they are also interested in subjects such as media studies.

Education and Health Data

- 🗁 Life expectancy at birth, male: 75.2
- 🗁 Life expectancy at birth, female: 81.2
- 🗁 Infant mortality rate per 1,000: 4
- 🗁 Under five mortality rate per 1,000: 5
- 🗁 Physicians per 1,000 people: 3.3
- 🗁 Health expenditure as % of GDP: 10.8%
- 🗁 Education expenditure as % of GDP: 4.5%
- 🗁 Primary school net enrollment: 87%
- 🗁 Student-teacher ratio, primary: 14.8
- 🗁 Adult literacy as % of age 15+: 99

Source: United Nations Agencies and World Bank

Focus on: Vocational Training

Vocational training combines on-the-job training with more formal classes. Germans regard qualifications—educational awards that are broader than just academic degrees—as very important. All students in German schools are expected to work for a qualification. In this way, vocational training has the same prestige as academic education. Specialized vocational schools called *Berufschulen* have been set up throughout the country to ensure that vocational training in Germany is of the highest quality. These schools specialize in training for a specific trade, such as carpentry or plumbing.

HEALTH CARE

Germany has an extensive and efficient health care system, which is largely privately funded. All towns over a certain size have a hospital, and most have emergency rooms to deal with accidents and emergencies. Ambulances are fast and efficient, even in rural areas. Citizens from other EU countries receive free first aid and emergency health care, but there are charges for other medical services. A network of local doctors provide most treatments. Except for major operations, it is unusual for a patient to go to a hospital for treatment except in an emergency. Instead, people pay to go to a doctor in private practice. Doctors make diagnoses and write prescriptions, which have to be taken to a pharmacist.

Germany has suffered from the spread of the HIV/AIDS virus. In 2004, it had forty-one thousand people living with this disease. About 660 people in the country die from AIDS-related illnesses each year, but improved treatments and more specialized treatment departments in hospitals have been introduced.

A network of dentists in private practice serves the local population. They carry out almost all dental treatments themselves in their offices. Again, emergency treatment is free for people from EU countries, but there are charges for additional treatments.

ALTERNATIVE MEDICINE

Germans are very health conscious. Pharmacies in Germany offer a wide range of alternative or complementary medicines, including homeopathic treatments. Special spas and hotels have opened to give people a choice of services including mud baths, brine baths, and detoxification programs.

Diets are popular in Germany, where about 20 percent of people are classified as obese. Obesity in Germany is particularly common among young people and is the result of a diet often based on foods high in fats and salt and a lifestyle that is largely inactive. With the creation of fitness trails (*Trimm-dich-Pfade*) in parks and wooded areas of towns in Germany, people are being encouraged to exercise more.

▲ People in Berlin and other German cities light candles on World AIDS Day to remember those who have died from the disease.

OPPORTUNITIES FOR EXERCISE

During the winter, skiing—especially cross-country skiing (*Langlauf*)—is a popular form of exercise for many people in Germany. Germans also like to play soccer and cycle. Special cycling trails in towns and across country areas encourage people to cycle to work.

In an effort to improve the health and wellness of Germany's people, city planners have created green spaces in heavily built-up areas such as the Ruhr. In the 1990s, when coal mines closed in the Ruhr, the local planners took the opportunity to develop parks with wooded areas and fitness trails. In total, twenty-seven million trees were planted in the Ruhr between 1980 and 1999.

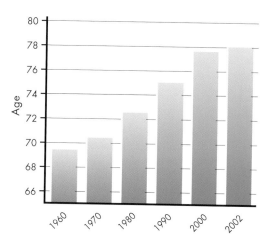

▲ Life expectancy at birth, 1960–2002

 Did You Know?

The most common cause of death in Germany is heart attacks. Heart disease is largely caused by a diet that is too rich in fats and salt and by a lack of exercise. The next most common cause of death in the country is cancer.

 Did You Know?

Many places in Germany have lifts and ramps for the benefit of wheelchair users. The country has fewer facilities for people with disabilities such as deafness and blindness.

▼ Many German cities have fitness trails so that people can get the daily exercise they need to stay healthy.

CHAPTER 11

Culture and Religion

Germany holds numerous festivals and celebrations, many of them dating back to pre-Christian and medieval times. At the famous Oktoberfest in Munich, large quantities of beer and wurst are consumed in celebration of a successful harvest. On Easter Sunday, children search their gardens for Easter eggs hidden by their parents. One of the country's most recently introduced celebrations takes place each year on October 3. On this day, Germans organize parades and fairs to commemorate their country's reunification.

▼ In Bavaria, people wear traditional costumes and join in festivals of music and dancing on May Day.

A MUSICAL HERITAGE

Germany has a rich history in music. Johann Sebastian Bach (1685–1750) wrote famous concertos, cantatas, and religious music, including settings of the *Passion*. During about the same time, another German composer, Georg Friedrich Handel (1685–1759) wrote operas, instrumental works, and church music, including the famous *Messiah*. Ludwig van Beethoven (1770–1827) composed many famous symphonies, in spite of losing his hearing in 1819. Other major German composers include Johannes Brahms (1833–1897) and Robert Schumann (1810–1856), both of whom are famous for their romantic piano music.

PLAYWRIGHTS, NOVELISTS, AND POETS

One of the most famous German writers is Johann Wolfgang von Goethe (1749–1832), who wrote poetry, plays, and novels. His most famous play, *Faust*, tells the tale of a man who sells his soul to the devil in exchange for knowledge and power. Friedrich von Schiller (1759–1805) worked with Goethe and wrote plays such as *The Maid of Orleans* and *William Tell*. Other important German authors include Thomas Mann (1875–1955), who won the Nobel Prize for Literature in 1929. Mann's writings focused on the problem of the artist in middle-class society, and his works include *Dr. Faustus* and the short story *Death in Venice*.

Bertolt Brecht (1898–1956) wrote novels, plays, and poetry and produced plays for the theater. In the 1930s, his communist sympathies made him a target for the Nazis and he was forced into exile in the United States. He wrote scripts Hollywood but left the United States for East Germany in 1947, where his communist beliefs found favor. Günter Grass (1927–) is a more recent German author of novels, poetry, and plays that are critical of modern society.

 Did You Know?

Albert Einstein was a German physicist who developed the theory of relativity. He was awarded the Nobel Prize in 1921. Einstein moved to the United States in 1933 and became an American citizen in 1940. In 1932, Werner Heisenberg, another German physicist, won the Nobel Prize for his research on hydrogen.

Focus on: Marlene Dietrich

Marlene Dietrich was born Marie Magdalene von Losch in Berlin in 1901. She went to acting school, then worked in German silent films in the 1920s. In 1930, she became world famous as a seductive cabaret singer in the German film *Der Blaue Engel* (*The Blue Angel*) and was quickly signed to Paramount Studios in Hollywood. After moving to the United States, she became a major star. Her success was based on her sophisticated, mysterious presence as an actress. In 1937, she became a U.S. citizen. A committed anti-Nazi, Dietrich performed for the Allied troops during World War II. After 1945, she made a few well-attended public appearances and took the leading role in a handful of carefully chosen films. She died in Paris at the age of 90.

▲ A statue of writer and poet Johann Wolfgang von Goethe in Berlin marks his major achievements as one of the first important German writers.

ARCHITECTURAL ACHIEVEMENTS

Germany has buildings in a wide range of architectural styles. These include buildings in the Gothic style that dates from 1200, when cathedrals such as Cologne and Magdeburg were built to dominate the surrounding areas. The Baroque period, which began in the seventeenth century, led to the construction

▼ Berlin's Sony Center is one of the many new offices and apartment buildings constructed since the reunification of the country.

of some giant castles, such as Karlsruhe Castle, which also dominated their surroundings. In the eighteenth century, the strict geometry of the neoclassical style produced structures such as the Brandenburg Gate, which is based on a Greek design. In the nineteenth century, longer spans of glass were used in buildings. This use of glass resulted from the introduction of steel, with its great supporting strength. Members of the Art Nouveau movement used large spans of glass to create beautiful windows in department stores such as the Wertheim store in Berlin. The Bauhaus movement, developed in the twentieth century and led by Walter Gropius, designed objects and buildings in ways that stressed their functions. More recently, older buildings in Germany, such as the Museuminsel in Berlin, are being restored, and new glass and steel constructions such as the Sony Center are appearing on the skyline.

ARTISTS

In Germany, the impact of the Renaissance, which occurred in the fifteenth century, is best seen in the paintings of Albrecht Dürer (1471–1528). Dürer produced many drawings of nature and animals in exact detail. Much of his work is still on display in museums in Munich. Later, Max Liebermann (1847–1945) was a forerunner of the impressionist school of painting in Germany.

 Did You Know?

Aachen Cathedral, Cologne Cathedral, and Speyer Cathedral are UNESCO World Heritage sites. This means that a branch of the United Nations considers them worthy of continued preservation because of their historical value.

DIFFERENT FAITHS

Christianity is the main religion in Germany, and its two main branches, Protestantism and Catholicism, share roughly the same number of worshippers. The German constitution guarantees religious freedom to all. The division of the country into a mostly Catholic south and a mostly Protestant north dates back to the Peace of Augsburg (1555), which allowed the ruler of each state to choose the religion that would be paramount within his or her state. Immigration has also affected the distribution of religions in the country. The arrival of French Huguenots in the late seventeenth century, for example, gave a big boost to the Protestant population of Berlin.

In 2003, followers of Islam made up 2 percent of the German population. Most members of Germany's Islamic population are Turkish former guest workers who have now settled permanently in the country. The country's main Islamic centers are Dortmund, Dusseldorf, Frankfurt, and Essen.

Before World War II, about 530,000 Jews lived in Germany. The Holocaust and emigration devastated the country's Jewish community. Jewish emigrants from the former Soviet Union, however, have increased the number of Jews living in Germany in recent years. About eleven thousand Jews now live in Germany, more than five thousand of whom came from the former Soviet Union. The largest groups are in Berlin, Munich, and Frankfurt-am-Main.

▲ The synagogue at Worms is the oldest synagogue in Europe. It is a reminder of the importance of Jews in the history of Germany.

? Did You Know?

Germans who belong to a recognized religious denomination have to pay a church tax of 9 percent of their income.

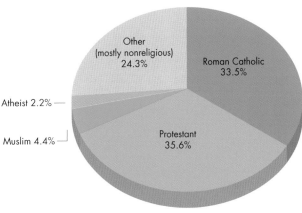

Other (mostly nonreligious) 24.3%

Roman Catholic 33.5%

Atheist 2.2%

Muslim 4.4%

Protestant 35.6%

▲ Germany's major religions

CHAPTER 12

Leisure and Tourism

▲ Germans sailing in Hamburg. As Germans have become wealthier, they have gained more leisure time and the means to enjoy sports such as sailing.

Sports are an important part of German life. People enjoy taking part in or watching a range of sports, from soccer and cycling to sailing and skiing. In school, special classes above and beyond the normal physical education lessons help pupils develop their sports skills from an early age. A wide range of gyms and other facilities encourage people to keep active later in life.

 Did You Know?

The Bergen-Belsen memorial lies 35 miles (60 km) northeast of Hanover on the grounds of former Nazi prisoner of war (POW) and concentration camps. The memorial has marked graves and monuments to remind people of the suffering and deaths that occurred in the camps between 1940 and 1945 under the Nazi regime. A documentation center provides visitors with a history of the camp and its victims.

SOCCER

On a typical winter weekend in Germany, more than 300,000 people throughout the country watch soccer matches. The *Bundeslegia* (Soccer League) of Germany is important in Europe. German teams also take part in the Champions League of Europe every year. The Champions League is a competition between the top teams from each European soccer league.

In their leisure time, Germans are very social and enjoy visits to their families. They also like going to cafes, where they consume rich pastries, cakes, coffee, and herbal teas, and going to the movies. Gardening is a popular hobby, and Germany has many garden centers offering a wide range of plants.

SPA TOWNS

Tourism in Germany has ancient roots. The Romans had resorts such as Aachen, where the rich could go to relax. In the eighteenth century, spa towns such as Baden Baden became popular. The water in these spas was believed to have medicinal qualities, and drinking it was thought to cure a range of illnesses. Wealthy Germans visited the spas with the hope of benefiting from the waters.

In the nineteenth century, mountain climbing in Germany became popular, and people from all over Europe converged on the peaks of the Alps, such as the Zugspitze (9,721 feet/2,963 m) in Bavaria. People also visited the mountains to enjoy the clean, clear air and the beautiful scenery. Sea bathing also became popular in the nineteenth century. At first, rich aristocrats traveled to the Baltic coast to enjoy the sand and the sea. Later, middle-class tourists came,

as well. The increasing number of railway lines made it possible for many more people to travel all over Germany and Europe throughout the nineteenth and twentieth centuries.

▲ The water of the spa at Baden Baden is said to have healing powers. People bathe in the waters of this spa to ease muscular and arthritic pain.

Focus on: Berlin

Berlin is a site of great historical importance in Germany because of its postwar history. In 1961, the Berlin Wall was built, dividing communist East Germany from capitalist West Germany. The Wall was built across streets, and houses were demolished to make way for it. Families were split up, and sometimes did not see one another for many years. Checkpoint Charlie was a famous place at which people were stopped to show their identification papers when crossing from one side of Berlin to the other.

HISTORIC TOWNS

More recently, cheap air travel has allowed more people to visit Germany's attractions. Historic towns such as Heidelberg, Cologne, and Dresden attract many tourists, as does the picturesque valley of the Rhine River, with its castles and gorges. In addition to coastal resorts and spa towns, Germany has vibrant cities such as Berlin and Hamburg. The museums, bars, and nightlife of these cities attract thousands of visitors. Some visitors to Germany's cities are people attending business conferences. These travelers make an important contribution to the economies of the cities they visit.

▼ Tourists visit the new glass dome of the Reichstag, which reopened in 1999 in Berlin. The dome provides a viewing gallery and represents Germany's commitment to "transparency" in government.

Germans themselves are enthusiastic about traveling abroad. Many Germans visit the neighboring countries of Switzerland and Austria, where people speak the German language. These countries have great resources for winter sports and summer hiking. Millions of Germans also travel to enjoy the warmth and sunshine of the Mediterranean area. Countries such as Spain, Portugal, Turkey, Egypt, and Tunisia are especially popular with Germans, and many own second homes in these countries.

IMPACT OF TOURISM

The growth of tourism in Germany has created some environmental and social issues. For example, the influx of a large number of tourists can change the social structure of a small town. Once the visitors arrive, local businesses become geared toward the tourist

industry. At some of Germany's major tourist sites, such as Unter den Linden, in Berlin, or Garmisch-Partenkirchen, in Bavaria, local people appear to have no other function than to act as guides or salespeople.

In rural areas, environmental issues can arise because of tourism. For example, the popularity of winter skiing in the Bavarian Alps has led to the creation of an increasing number of ski runs. The clearing of land for skiing, in turn, has reduced vegetation cover on the mountain-sides and exposed the soil to erosion by wind and water.

The growth of tourism in Germany, however, has many benefits. Tourism is a major industry, and millions of Germans depend on it for their livelihoods. New jobs have been created in hotels, restaurants, and nightclubs in Berlin and other large cities. Jobs have also been created in

villages and towns outside the major cities, such as Rudesheim in the scenic Rhine Valley. People are employed driving taxis, acting as ski guides, and making and selling souvenirs.

▲ The Alps in Bavaria are one of the best areas for skiing in Germany. They are high enough to have snow and ice for more than four months of the year.

Did You Know?

Christmas fairs are very popular in Germany, and those in Munich, Berlin, Münster, and Heidelberg are famous. They attract visitors from other European countries, as well as Germans doing their Christmas shopping.

Tourism in Germany

- 🗁 Tourist arrivals, millions: 17.969
- 🗁 Earnings from tourism in U.S. $: 19,158,000,000
- 🗁 Tourism as % foreign earnings: 3
- 🗁 Tourist departures, millions: 73.3
- 🗁 Expenditure on tourism in U.S. $: 53,196,000,000

Source: World Bank

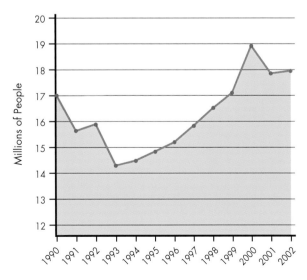

▲ Changes in international tourism, 1990–2001

CHAPTER 13

Environment and Conservation

The growth of Germany's towns, villages, industrial sector, and population has put pressure on the country's environment. Relatively few places in the country have escaped the impact of people and their works. Land is still being lost to new roads, airports, factories, and housing developments. Many river courses have been changed in order to create internal shipping routes. Many other watercourses have little life in them, showing the impact of past pollution by factories and cities. Air pollution drifts into Germany from neighboring countries such as Poland and the Czech Republic, both of which had less strict environmental protection laws when they were controlled by communist governments.

▼ In spite of years of legislation and progress in environmental pollution control, factories like this one near Berlin still cause air-pollution problems.

IMPROVING STANDARDS

Most Germans are aware of the importance of protecting their environment, and much progress has been made in improving environmental standards. Catalytic converters, which reduce pollution, have been put in most German vehicles. Since 2001, the EU has required that catalytic converters be included in all vehicles. Levels of some pollutants, such as carbon monoxide, have been halved as a result of the new measures. To encourage more people to use public transportation, the German government places an ecological tax on gasoline. This tax money is used to develop public transportation in the country, such as new or more regular bus services, or to develop integrated bus and train centers to make transfer between different modes of transportation easier. In spite of these efforts, some cities still have smog alerts in the summer.

Environmental and Conservation Data

📁 Forested area as % total land area: 15

📁 Protected area as % total land area: 31.7

📁 Number of protected areas: 7,607

SPECIES DIVERSITY

Category	Known species	Threatened species
Mammals	76	11
Breeding birds	247	5
Reptiles	16	n/a
Amphibians	20	n/a
Fish	95	6
Plants	2,682	12

Source: World Resources Institute

POLLUTION OF THE SEAS

In 1988, eighteen thousand dead seals washed ashore on the North Sea coast of Germany. Scientific research established that the seals had died as a result of pollution of the seas by metals such as lead, zinc, and mercury. These metals weakened the immune systems of the seals and made them prone to a range of viruses.

Germany is one of the countries around the North Sea that has reduced pollution from metals, fertilizers, pesticides, and phosphates in an attempt to improve conditions for seals and forms of sea life. So far, this process seems to be working, and the North Sea is cleaner now than it has been at any time since the 1970s.

◀ Since the 1990s, trams have become an important form of transportation in German cities. Trams provide quiet, fast, and pollution-free transportation, and this has made them popular with many people.

In the 1970s and 1980s, Germany's rivers—especially the Rhine—were so badly polluted that parts of them were declared hazards to human health. These environmental disasters spurred the government into producing whole-river plans designed to improve water quality in both the Rhine and the Elbe. These plans have greatly reduced the pollution of the country's rivers by farms, factories, and cities. A measure of the success of these plans is the fact that, in 1997, salmon and sea trout were found in the Rhine for the first time in fifty years.

Did You Know?

The environmental group Greenpeace is very active in Germany. In the 1990s, Greenpeace protesters successfully prevented the Shell Oil company from sinking an old oil platform in the North Sea.

RESTORING WATER MEADOWS

In 2000, a plan called High Water on the River Rhine was set up. This plan aims to reduce flood damage by restoring former water meadows that used to help absorb the impact of flooding. It is hoped that this program will be completed by the year 2020. The program works by paying farmers to leave fields in flood plain areas as traditional water meadows rather than plowing them.

Did You Know?

The golden eagle has again begun to breed in some of the Alpine areas of Germany.

▼ Walkers in a German forest in 1998 are surrounded by evidence of acid rain damage to trees.

ACID RAIN

One environmental problem that Germany is overcoming is acid rain. All rain contains some acid because gases in the air, such as sulphur dioxide, dissolve in water. In the last twenty years, rain in many areas has become more acidic because the amount of sulphur dioxide in the air has increased. Acid rain damages plants, especially trees where the new growth can be destroyed and the whole tree may die. Acid rain also kills fish and plants in lakes and rivers. In Germany, special filters that catch sulphur and nitrogen gases are fitted to power stations in order to prevent acid rain. In addition, German industry is now using gas, rather than coal, to fuel power stations, because it yields fewer dangerous gases. Germany's government introduced these measures in the 1980s. Since then, some improvement of the water quality of lakes and rivers has occurred. Damage to trees from acid rain is still a problem.

IMPROVEMENTS IN WILDLIFE PROTECTION

In spite its remaining problems, Germany has been successful in improving its environment. In the forests of Bavaria and in the east of the country, wild boar, wolves, adders, and deer are starting to increase in numbers. Similarly, in the Alpine areas, chamois, a type of deer, and ibex, a type of goat, are multiplying rapidly. Other animals such as the beaver, the horseshoe bat, and the eagle owl—which in the 1980s were threatened with extinction—are now enjoying special protection.

Germany's national parks were created to protect and preserve wildlife, plants, and areas of outstanding natural beauty. It was feared that the expansion of farms, mines, and towns would threaten the existence of these areas. Today, these parks are carefully controlled and monitored to ensure that nothing damages or destroys their natural attractions.

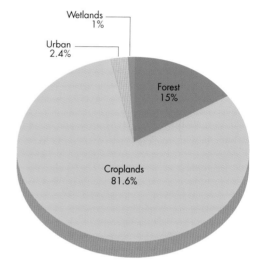

▲ Habitat type as percentage of total area

▲ The European wolf was hunted almost to extinction in Germany, but it is now making a comeback in some of the country's national parks.

CHAPTER 14

Future Challenges

Germany has changed a great deal since its first unification in 1871. It suffered division between 1945 and 1990 but then was reunified to its present size and shape. In spite of all these dramatic changes, Germany has become a rich, influential country, and the German people enjoy a high standard of living.

REINTEGRATION

Challenges for the future still exist for Germany. First, Germany must successfully complete the reintegration of the eastern areas with the rest of the country. Much progress has been made in terms of building new roads, railroads, and infrastructure. Eastern farms and villages have been modernized, and factories have been rebuilt, re-equipped, and reorganized. Much remains to be achieved, however, in reducing unemployment and rebuilding infrastructure in the eastern region.

Second, because of Germany's aging population and shrinking workforce, there will be fewer people of working age to support the growing

▼ Young people growing up in eastern Germany today are finding it easier to adapt to the way their country has changed than are their parents and grandparents, who grew up in a divided country.

number of older people. In the future, Germany may need to allow more immigrants to enter the country to provide the necessary workforce. Problems may arise because these new immigrants would not necessarily be able to gain German citizenship.

Third, Germany needs to continue focusing on environmental improvement. Environmental awareness has increased in the last ten years, and the country has made progress with issues such as domestic recycling, the establishment of national parks and protected areas, and the use of catalytic converters in vehicles. Nevertheless, of the one hundred or so mammals on the country's list of endangered species, about one-third are still in danger of dying out, including shrews and field mice.

A COMPETITIVE ECONOMY

Economically, the country has not enjoyed the rapid growth of the 1960s and 1970s, mainly because of the costs of redeveloping the eastern regions. In the future, an increasing amount of the country's wealth is likely to be derived from service industries, such as finance and tourism, and high-tech industries, such as computer manufacturing. The challenge here is to develop these industries in ways that enable them to compete successfully with other suppliers of global services and high-tech products, such as the United States, Japan, and China.

CENTRAL ROLE IN THE EU

Germany's economic and political power and influence within the expanded European Union will provide a good platform from which it can meet these various challenges. Within the EU, Germany continues to drive forward the movement to a single European currency and is encouraging more EU members to adopt the

▲ An aging population means that Germany may encounter health-care and pension problems in the future.

euro. Germany is still developing its relationship with Russia and attempting to bring Russia and Europe closer together on economic and political issues. Globally, Germany sees itself as the "conscience" of the EU. It opposed the invasion of Iraq in 2003 and is eager to help the EU develop its foreign policy. Germany continues to speak out about the need for a united approach to issues such as terrorism. It is also eager to extend its influence in the Far East, especially in China, which it sees as the major force for change in that region.

Time Line

First century B.C. Clashes between German tribes and the Romans.

742-814 B.C. Charlemagne rules most of Germany and unites the country.

1348-50 Black Death kills one-third of the German population.

1358 The Hanseatic League, a commercial association of German towns, is formed to trade between northern and southern Europe.

1517 Martin Luther starts the Reformation.

1618-1648 The Thirty Years' War ravages Germany.

1763 Prussia triumphs over Austria in the Seven Years' War and lays claim to part of Poland.

1806 Prussia is captured by Napoleon Bonaparte.

1815 Germany becomes a confederation of thirty-five states.

1871 Unification of Germany.

1914-18 World War I.

1920-30 Economic collapse and hyper-inflation in Germany.

1933 Adolf Hitler becomes chancellor of Germany, and the Nazi party comes to power.

1939-45 World War II, at the end of which Germany surrenders.

1946 Germany is divided into a communist East and a capitalist West.

1948 and 1950 East Germany confirms alliances with the Soviet Union.

1953 Revolt in East Germany is put down by troops.

1959 West Germany is a founding member of the European Economic Community (EEC), the forerunner of the European Union.

1960-70 West German economy grows strongly, and consumer goods are cheap.

1970 A sharp rise in terrorism in West Germany, with the abduction and assassination of political figures.

1980-90 A steep increase in the cost of consumer goods in East Germany.

August 1989 Massive emigration from East to West Germany. Churches lead opposition to the communist regime.

November 1989 Berlin Wall is breached.

August 1990 East and West Germany are reunified.

2000 Germany celebrates ten years of reunification.

2005 The European Union is enlarged to twenty-five members.

Glossary

baroque a style of ornamental architecture and decoration, popular in Europe from the late sixteenth to the early eighteenth century

capital accumulated or inherited wealth

capitalism an economic system in which the means of production, distribution, and exchange are in private hands

Celts a people whose first known territory was in central Europe in about 1200 B.C., and later spread throughout most of Europe

cog railway a railway used in mountain areas in which a central cog beneath the train is engaged to help it climb steep slopes

communism an economic system in which the means of production, distribution, and exchange are in the hands of the state

communist a follower of communism

constitute to make up or compose

directives instructions or orders

federation the union of several states, generally for political or administrative reasons

Franks Germanic peoples living in Europe between the third and tenth centuries A.D.

gross domestic product (GDP) total value of goods and services produced within the borders of a country

gross national income (GNI) total value of a country's income from goods and services produced by its residents both within the country and elsewhere in the world

Huns a wandering people that invaded the Roman Empire in the fifth century A.D.

Industrial Revolution a series of economic changes based on the use of new machinery and steam power in factories. It started in Britain in the 1760s and spread to the rest of Europe and, later, much of the world

infrastructure the network of roads, railways, canals, water, and electricity supplies necessary for the successful running of factories, offices, shops, and houses

Lombardy a region of northern Italy that includes Lake Como and the capital of which is Milan

papal state an area of central Italy in which a pope was the ruler from 756 to 1870 A.D.

plenary relating to assemblies or councils

Prussia a state in northern Germany which became the center for the unification of Germany in the nineteenth century

sand spit a tongue-shaped area of sand deposited by the sea a short distance offshore

silicon an element occurring in sand, quartz, granite, feldspar, and clay, that is used in the manufacture of solar cells

Soviet Union a huge communist state in eastern Europe that existed between 1917 and 1990 but ended with the downfall of communism. Following this, the Soviet Union was divided into separate independent nations

water meadow a meadow that stays fertile because it is flooded from time to time by a river or stream

Further Information

BOOKS TO READ

Berlin (*Great Cities of the World* series)
Nicola Barber
(World Almanac Library)

The Berlin Wall (*Building World Landmarks* series)
Debbie Levy
(Blackbirch Press)

Causes of World War II (*20th-Century Perspectives* series)
Paul Dowswell
(Heinemann Library)

European Union
(*International Organizations* series)
Petra Press
(World Almanac Library)

The Fall of the Berlin Wall
(*Days That Changed the World* series)
Jeremy Smith
(World Almanac Library)

Germany (*Discovering Cultures* series)
Sharon Gordon
(Marshall Cavendish)

Germany (*True Book* series)
Susan Heinrichs Gray
(Children's Press)

Life and Death in Hitler's Europe
Jane Shuter
(Heinemann Library)

USEFUL WEB SITES

Bergen Belsen
www.bergen-belsen.de/en/

Berlin Wall
www.wall-berlin.org/gb/berlin.htm

Federal Statistical Office of Germany
www.destatis.de/e_home.htm

German Embassy
www.germany-info.org/relaunch/index.html

History for Kids
www.historyforkids.org/learn/germans/
index.htm

Hope, Anguish, and the Berlin Wall
www.microsoft.com/mscorp/artcollection/
exhibitions/august/

MoMA - Artists of Brücke
www.moma.org/exhibitions/2002/brucke/

Museum of Tolerance Online
motlc.wiesenthal.com

World Almanac for Kids Online:
www.worldalmanacforkids.com/explore/
nations/germany.html

The World Factbook
www.odci.gov/cia/publications/factbook/
geos/gm.html

Index

Page numbers in **bold**
indicate pictures.

abortion 25
air travel 40, **40**, 52
Alps, the 14, 15, 16, 17, **17**, 51, 53, **53**
alternative medicine 44
animals 55, 56, 57, **57**, 59
architecture 48, **48**
art 48
asylum seekers 20, 21
Attila the Hun 8

Bach, Johann Sebastian 6, 46
Baltic coast 4, 6, 14, **14**, 15, 28, 29, 51
barges 40, **41**
Bavaria **5**, 6, 16, 22, **46**, 51, 53, **53**, 57
beer 31, 46
Beethoven, Ludwig von 6, 46
Bergen-Belsen 50
Berlin 4, 6, 10, **10**, **12**, 13, **13**, 17, 18, 22, 33, **33**, 39, 40, **44**, 47, **47**, 48, **48**, 49, 51, 52, **52**, 53, **54**
Berlin Wall 12, 13, **13**, 51
Bismarck, Otto von 4, 10
Black Forest 6, 16, 17, **29**
Bonaparte, Napoleon 9
Brahms, Johannes 46
Brecht, Bertolt 47
bubonic plague 9

Celts 8
Charlemagne 8, **8**
chemicals industry 5, 10, 26, 33, **33**
citizenship 21, 59
climate 16, **16**, 17, **17**
coal 5, 10, 26, **26**, 40

Cold War, the 13, 35
collectivization 12
communism 12, 13, 35, 38, 47, 51, 54
concentration camps 11, **11**
co-operatives 5, 31
culture 4, 46, **46**, 47, **47**, 48, 49

Dietrich, Marlene 47
Dresden 11, 15, **24**, 52
Dürer, Albrecht 48

East Germany (German Democratic Republic) 5, 12, 13, 18, 19, 24, 25, 31, 32, 38, 41, 47, 51
economy 5, 30, 31, 32, 33, 35, **35**, 59
education 42, **42**, 43, **43**
Einstein, Albert 6, 47
energy 26, **26**, 27, **27**, 28, **28**, 29
engineering industry 5, 10, 32
environmental problems 26, 27, 28, 33, 41, 54, **54**, 55, **55**, 56, **56**, 57, 59
European Central Bank 35, **35**
European Monetary Union (EMU) 13, 35
European Union (EU) 4, 34, **34**, 35, 44, 54, 59
exports 36, 37

farming 30, **30**, 31, **31**
festivals 46, **46**
fishing 29
fitness trails 44, **45**
floods 15, 56
Frankfurt-am-Main 18, 33, 37, 39, 40, 49
Franks 8

Goethe, Johann Wolfgang von 6, 47, **47**
government 5, **12**, 22, **22**, 23, **23**
Grass, Günter 47
Greenpeace 56
Gropius, Walter 48
guest workers 20, 21

Hamburg 19, 39
Handel, Georg Friedrich 46
health care 20, 44, 45
Heidegger, Martin 6
Heidelberg **6**, 42, **43**, 52, 53
history 4, 8, **8**, 9, 10, **10**, 11, **11**, 12, **12**, 13, **13**
Hitler, Adolf 11, 32
HIV/AIDS 44, **44**
Holocaust, the 11, **11**, 49
Holy Roman Empire 8, 9
hydro-electricity 27

immigration 20, 59
imports 5, 36, 37
Industrial Revolution 10
industrialization 10, 11
international finance 37
iron 5, 40

Jews 11, 49, **49**

Kant, Immanuel 6
kindergarten 42, **42**
Kohl, Helmut 13, 24

landscapes **5**, 14, **14**, 15, **15**
leisure activities 50, **50**, 51, **51**, 52, 53

Liebermann, Max 48
lignite 5, 26
Luther, Martin 8

Mann, Thomas 47
manufacturing industries 5, 32, 36, 37
Marx, Karl 6
minerals 29
music 6, 46
Muslims **21**, 49

national parks 57, 59
Nazi Party (National Socialist Party) 10, **10**, 11, 47
North Atlantic Treaty Organization (NATO) 13, 35
North Sea 4, 14, 28, 29

Peace of Augsburg 49
politics 4, 24, 25, **25**
pollution 26, 27, 28, 33, 41, 54, **54**, 55, **55**, 56, **56**, 57
population 18, 19, 20, 21, 58

Protestantism 9, **9**, 49
Prussia 4, 9, 10

railways 39, **39**, 51, 58
Reformation 8-9
renewable energy sources 27, **27**, 28, **28**
reunification 5, 13, 24, 25, 31, 32, 46, 58
rivers 6, 14, 15, **15**, 27, 31, 33, 40, **41**, 52, 56
roads 11, 38, **38**, 39, 58
Roman Catholicism 8, 9, 49
Romans 8, 51
Rügen 14
Ruhr, the 26, 40, 45

Schiller, Fredrich von 6, 47
Schumann, Robert 46
service industries 33, 59
spas 44, 51, **51**, 52
sports **19**, 45, 50, **50**, 51, 53, **53**
steel-making industry 5, 10
Stuttgart 18

telecommunications 41
temperatures 16, 17
Thirty Years' War 9
timber industry 28-29, **29**
tourism 33, **40**, 51, 52, **52**, 53, 59
trade 35, 36, **37**
traffic congestion 41
transportation 38, **38**, 39, **39**, 40, **40**, 41, **41**, 54, **55**

unification 10, 58

vocational training 43

West Germany (Federal Republic of Germany) 5, 12, 13, 19, 25, 38, 51
wine production 31, **31**
women 24, 25
World War I 10
World War II 11, 35, 38, 47, 49